CW01431337

Plastic Viking Helmets

a selection of my poems

Andy Sutton

Cover conceived and created by Andy Sutton.

Andy Sutton is a Nottingham based poet who writes poems that rhyme and all that. Mostly.

Sully is a Nottingham based dog who enjoys treats, walks, and pubs. He also poses reluctantly for book cover photos and features in some poems that rhyme and all that. Mostly.

Social media - The same things are posted to all accounts. There is more of a community on my Facebook page.
- Facebook: facebook.com/andysuttonpoetry
- Instagram: @andysuttonpoetry
- Twitter: @AndySutPoetry

Plastic Viking Helmets

For my two wonderful children.

Love and thanks to Sue for advice, support, and for steering me through my doubts. And for being Sue.

Andy

Contents

Start Of My Book

So here you are at the start of my book

If you expected a yarn you're mistook

These are just pages and pages of rhymes

Nearly all humour but sober sometimes

Not like the ones that you studied at school

With an exam that you failed like a fool

Pure entertainment with nothing to lose

This is a book that it's quite safe to choose

I'd like to think that you'll read and you'll smile

If you engage with these pages awhile

If thinking of buying I hope that you do

If you did already I'd like to thank you

Please enjoy.

Andy Sutton

If You

If you were on a mountain
I'd fly
If you were on a market
I'd buy
If you were needing intel
I'd spy
If you were washing dishes
I'd dry
If you were in a hard place
I'd try
If you were feeling sadness
I'd sigh
If you were wanting junk food
I'd fry
If you needed a wherefore
I'd why
If you needed excuses
I'd lie
If you were heading elsewhere
I'd cry

Places For Poetry

Sometimes people ask of me
Where can they write poetry
I will say quite honestly
Anywhere you seem to be

Sitting on your grandma's knee
Perched securely up a tree
In a garden drinking tea
Prison (if the guards agree)

While you watch a DVD
Waiting for a jubilee
Just before a spending spree
Down in Memphis, Tennessee

Sipping rather fine Chablis
On a cruise ship to Capri
After all we say, don't we
Verse things happen when at sea

Pun Porn

Oxford secret agents sleeping

Those are dreaming spiers

Having lots of tools for gripping

Sounds like multi pliers

Jacob Rees Mogg on volcanos

That's a lava Tory

Add a new floor to the car park

That's another storey

L.I.B.

I drum for the Rolling Stones

I invented mobile phones

I have flown around the moon

I am getting up real soon

I'm lying

In bed

While I'm lying in bed

The Pit And Pentium

The Cross Keys and the Prince of Wales

The White Swan and White Hart

The Black Bull and The Seven Bales

Kings Arms and Horse and Cart

Old pub names can be quite sublime

Romantic some would say

Named after objects of their time

Routine things in their day

I'll help you paint the new town red

Not all pubs are the same

I recommend The Selfie's Head

Or Influence And Fame

I won't suggest your pals leave home

For The Alexa Bar

There's not much at The Google's Chrome

Less still The TikTok Star

The Facebook Tavern has some charms

The Mac has much to boast

Avoid The Phone and Tablet Arms

But try The Viral Post

There's good beer at The Blog and Meme

With monthly open mics

Then you might try The Song and Stream

Near The Ten Thousand Likes

Now when you've done that side of town

You'll want to try the best

My final tip to sink one down

The Data Stealer's Rest

Normal Dog

I wish he was a normal dog

Like Minx, and Nikos too

But Sully doesn't do the things

That all the others do

I drop food on the kitchen floor

A scrap he might enjoy

But does he leap to scoop it up?

No, not my Sully boy

I'm working hard and not aware

There's someone at the door

But does he bark or run around?

No, doesn't skip a snore

He needs to pee or needs to poo

He wants to be let out

But does he bark or make a sound?

No, stands there and says nowt

I put his food into his bowl

It's like I am his waiter

Devour it all? Picks chicken out

Then leaves the rest 'til later

I go up to the bathroom

To do what I must do

He follows me and watches

I think that's odd, don't you?

But then I think it's not all bad

He's friends with all he meets

He likes to be a good boy

Especially if there's treats

I'm glad he's not a normal dog

Upon reflecting fully

He's happy and contented

And most of all he's Sully

Pick A Side

Word nerd and grammar pedant

or

Bland herd and syntax sedent

Art Poem 1: Andy Warhol

```
   WARHOL              WARHOL
   VARIED              VARIED
   THINGS              THINGS
    VERY                VERY
  SLIGHTLY             LITTLE

   WARHOL              WARHOL
   VARIED              VARIED
   THINGS              THINGS
    ONLY                JUST
  SLIGHTLY            SLIGHTLY
```

Art Poem 2: Ceci N'est Pas Un Poème

You may know that in 1929 surrealist artist René Magritte unveiled his painting "The Treachery of Images". It's a very plain painting of a smokers' pipe, accompanied by the words "Ceci n'est pas une pipe" (This is not a pipe). His point was that you could not smoke this pipe, it is instead a painting.

Ceci n'est pas un poème
Despite how it appears
Just words arranged to look so
Or sound so in your ears

No this is not a poem
Magritte's was not a pipe
He said it's just a painting
Which caused a lot of hype

His painting's worth a fortune
I saw it at The Tate
I'll take this not-a-poem
And let them choose its fait

I hope they give me fortunes
Would ten thousand seem rash?
Or will I get a photo
Of piles and piles of cash?

Art Poem 3: Impressionist Poem

Impressionists painted q ite fast

To capture those things that don't last

They b oke formal rules

And some thought them fools

For severing links with the past

Art Poem 4: Mondrian Poem

```
REDREDREDREDBBLUEBLUEBLUE
REDREDREDREDLBLUEBLUEBLUE
REDREDREDREDABLUEBLUEBLUE
REDREDREDREDCBLUEBLUEBLUE
REDREDREDREDKBLUEBLUEBLUE
BLACKBLACKBLACKBLACKBLACK
BLUEBYELLOWBREDREDBYELLOW
BLUELYELLOWLREDREDLYELLOW
BLUEAYELLOWAREDREDAYELLOW
BLUECYELLOWCREDREDCYELLOW
BLUEKYELLOWKREDREDKYELLOW
```

Art Poem 5: Surrealist Poem

Surrealists are a funny sort

Delving in the brain

Drawing out the darkest thought

Questioning the sane

Mixing symbols from their dream

Paint the repressed wish

Things are rarely what they seem

Shooting carnal fish

Art Poem 6: Cubist Poem

There once were some cubists quite strange
Painted heads which they'd oddly arrange
An eye might get lost
But they'd charge a high cost
From a million you won't get much change

A Case Of Soup

Life is a minestrone

Say guys in 10cc

We're told by The Beatles the

Best things in life are free

The logical deduction

As anyone can see

Things in minestrone soup

Should not incur a fee

Tested this in Tesco and

The judge did not agree

The Companion

When I'm not feeling strong

You're there

When not getting along

You're there

When my life's gone wrong

You're there

Always by my side

The option suicide

You're there

Today Could Be The National Day For ...

Singing while we drive our cars
Looking up to see the stars
Finding money down a chair
Puddle jumps without a care
Loving UK's BBC
Loving grammar pedantry
Sending letters scribed by hand
TV screens in pubs being banned
Toilet humour, childish gags
Switching back to paper bags
Thanking cleaners, giving tips
Making things with paper clips
Speaking up without permission
Trying out a new position
Owning up that you were wrong
Playing loud a cheesy song
Dressing in outrageous clothes
Toppling rows of dominoes
Sharing poems that you like
Trying out at open mic
Telling jokes no-one will get
Cancelling all third world debt
Playing that old prog rock track
Wishing we had Hendrix back
Making noises with a comb
Hiding somewhere in your home

Home Olympics

Curling
Emma's hair gets her annoyed
Prepping for a date
She plugs in her heated tongs
So her hair's not straight

Shot put
Pouring out small vodka drinks
Into tiny glasses
Place it on my lips and flick
Down the throat it passes

Discus
When my grown up kids come round
Conscious of my years
We talk over future plans
Options, worries, fears

Bobsleigh
Uncle Robert, family rogue
Tends to irritate
Maybe we should bump him off
Seal his roguish fate

Archery
We listen to radio
Often BBC
While this play's not quite Ambridge
Sounds like it to me

One hundred metres
More than ninety nine at home
Smart one for the gas
Water and electric
Even body mass

Boxing
Listing things on auction sites
Selling coast to coast
Using lots of cardboard helps
Get them packed to post

Fencing
Aunty Jean's a business type
Ask-no-questions cheap
Sells things from her locked spare room
Where we may not peep

Relay
Carpet slides across our floor
Fitter wasn't bright
Need to take it all up then
Put it back just right

It's In The Post

Emma did a selfie
Posted it online
Eyebrows like a runway
Skin a funny shine
"This is me at Asda
Just about to pay."
Looks like thirteen others
Done by her today
Thirty two loves, twenty eight admiring comments

Alan's in the fan group
Of an old rock band
He moaned that the words are
Hard to understand
Likes the latest album
This will never do
Likes the song that charted
New vocalist too
Five hundred angry emojis, two thousand words of angry comments

"Never trust relations"
Lynn says in her feed
Does not share a detail
This is just a seed
Sibling? Parent? Partner?
Could give us the name
Could have told the story
But that's not her aim
*Twenty seven kissing emojis, twenty two comments, eighteen asking
what's wrong, thirteen include the word "hun" or "hugz"*

Raising our awareness
Jan used copy paste
This is so important
Don't scroll down in haste
Five percent will share this
Others never dare
What's the cause promoted?
Jan will never care
Eighty likes, fifty two supportive comments, ten shares, no action

Robert hates the Tories
All the things they do
Not forgiven Brexit
Anti vaxers too
Shares a Billy Bragg song
For the vibe it sends
This'll change the minds of
All his, erm, oh, lefty friends
Five thumbs up

Andy wrote a poem
Mocking Facebook posts
Dropped it in his newsfeed
No likes, no comments

I Really Don't Like Covid

Written during Covid lockdown

I really don't like Covid
It keeps me from the shops
No yellow label bargains
Until the virus stops

I really don't like Covid
It's keeping me from work
From laughing in the office
Where nasty germs may lurk

I really don't like Covid
It keeps me from the pub
From foaming beer and warming wine
And tasty bar snack grub

I really don't like Covid
It's keeping me from bands
From dancing, singing, stamping,
Cheering, clapping hands

I really don't like Covid
It's keeping me from friends
With coffee, chatting, laughing
And meals at the weekends

I really don't like Covid
And though these things are true
The main wrong done by Covid
Is keeping me from you

Mud

To teacher, to vet, and mortgage arranger

At best mud's a pain, at worst it's a danger

Mud, I would argue, has no pleasant features

Other than maybe for mud dwelling creatures

Any who walk by canals or on fields

Just don't like mud and the hazards it yields

Walking with muddy clothes certainly wrankles

I think I'll end up with a crust round my ankles

Feet try to edge round the side that's less damp

Earlier boots left no firm edge to tramp

Tense go my limbs as my foot starts to slide

Testing the concept of fall after pride

All nearby creatures then hear a loud thud

My bottom slapping in dastardly mud

Blue Pill

Written after the Conservative party suffered heavy local election defeat in May 2023

Blue pill for blue party that's now up the junction

After this case of electile dysfunction

The Amnesian King

On open plains of Amnese
Did beast roam wild and free
While sky ablaze with sunset
Lit river, field, and tree
King Kairlus was enchanted
And there did he decree
"Banquets shall be prepared here!
My people! Dine with me!"
Two leagues beyond the town wall
The site was named Partce
Built they great gilded feast halls
A spacious brewery
Kitchens, larders, tables, seats
And after new moons three
A night of merrymaking
Was planned by all with glee
The finest fare from harvest
And ale flowed endlessly
They danced and sang, imbibing
'Til dawn's light did they see
By morning did a queue form
In pain they seemed to be
With worried looks on faces
Some winced in agony
The queen looked on in wonder
Berate her king did she
"Have you forgotten toilets?
Your people need to pee."

Maths 1: The Minus Strike

Do you recall the minus strike

Of nineteen eighty four

You couldn't buy a takeaway

And sauce reduced no more

Photographers lost income

Despite their shutter clicks

A shortage of film negatives

Had stopped them printing pics

But logic came to rescue

The strike caused little fuss

By taking away minuses

They ended up with plus

Maths 2: Fraction Action

Used when we don't seek that whole
World denomination goal
Calculated risk rendition
Give no quarter to addition
Scaring pupils you are potent
Finally becoming quotient
Top and bottom with division
And for pi you're not precision
Ton below becomes percent
Good when n is different
Modulus is what will lurk
When division didn't work
Normally you have low topper
We say that it means you're proper
Vulgar though when more than one
Yet still there when half are gone
Many songs have fractions woven
Like that old Fifth of Beethoven
Meatloaf learned when just a lad
That Two Out Of Three Ain't Bad
At those odds he'd urge you risk it
Not whole like Half Man Half Biscuit
If Paradise Was Half As Nice
Half A Sixpence might suffice
Cutting into two not three
Made Eric The Half A Bee
Seeking integer distraction
Jagger got no satisfraction
Good for decimal rejection
You are fractional perfection

How Many Romans?

She rang the bell then asked the nurse

"It's Doctor Hill. Is Matt in?"

He looked at what she'd written down

and asked "What tongue is that in?"

She answered with a weary tone

"You'll find that's finest Latin.

In Rome the greatest minds spoke thus

to teach or have a spat in."

"I hesitate to mock" said he

"If I may throw my hat in

I'd say it seems a trifle grand

to just prescribe a statin."

Artificial Gravity

I could write for you about

The day they hurt my feelings

While someone else is mute about

Their bruises and their bleeding

Typing on my iPad

Write about my poverty

Grab me some attention

Artificial gravity

Divorcing My Species

That's it, I've had enough now
Don't try to reconcile
Human Race, you've worn me down
I'm single for a while

I don't think separation
Would help to heal us now
Let's go for decree nisi
And terminate our vow

We've had some happy times, yes
But now we're just not suited
I want to reach a settlement
Solicitors recruited

I'd like to have some access
But life apart is best
I'll keep the LP records
Then you can have the rest

It's not a no fault break up
The court will see I'm right
Unreasonable behaviour
The grounds that I will cite

When I've divorced my species
And ended this dispute
You'll see it's best for you too
Our decree absolute

Things To Be Made Illegal

Putting paper napkins on the plate under the snack

Cutting short by DJs of a long and classic track

Stickers on book covers that won't peel so cause a rip

Queue jumping and hailstones, drinks too hot to sip

Yappy dogs, and cities where they charge for public loos

Cutting public services that people need to use

Plastic cups for indoor drinks, fonts too small to see

Adding to a ticket price a further booking fee

Hanging On The Homophone

Bare just like a naked bear

Hair shaved from a well groomed hare

Bored by a blank notice board

Soared high with a flying sword

Flee the scene chased by a flea

See the world sailing the sea

Sold some shoes just newly soled

Cold because fire wasn't coaled

Here are sounds you need to hear

Dear like an expensive deer

Live And Let Tomorrow Never

A multi coloured herb that

James Bond wanted to try

Called for blue and pink but

He had no thyme to dye

Not to be defeated

He went out of his way

Visited the herb shop

To dye another day

Futility

Why can't I just focus on the

  things that make me glad?

Why waste any waking thoughts on

  things I wish I had?

Why do I spend money on the

  latest craze or fad?

Why do I watch movies that were

  made to make me sad?

Why do I read newspapers that

  amplify the bad?

Why read public comments that will

  only make me mad?

Minus, minus, minus, minus

  Why not add?

TWY

Time without you is hard to remember.

Time without you is hard.

To remember time without you is hard.

Without you time is hard.

Without you is hard.

Locations One, Two, And Three

Monday
Location one: a cordon
Police begin to search
Pretty woman, thirty-four
Gone missing after church
News tells us all about Gail
Blue purse in her pocket
Pink coat, red bag, a ham roll
Silver ring and locket

Location two: an alley
Up from the pizza place
Daniel exhales his last breath
With bruises on his face
Large bins were pulled around him
To hide him while he bled
Left there just after midnight
His T-shirt now stained red

Location three: a hallway
Where Penny kisses Joe
Then off to start their mornings
A hug before they go

Tuesday
Location one: no news yet
But social media grows
The speculation mounting
On what Gail's husband knows
Her smile all over tabloids
Tributes by the church door
Public join the searches
Police can do no more

Location two: it smells now
The scurrying of rats
No camera no witness
Except stray local cats

Location three: a hallway
Where Penny kisses Joe
Then off to start their mornings
A hug before they go

Wednesday
Location one: no updates
Location two: same way

Location three: repeating
A normal start of day
So Penny will walk Trudy
Who smelling ham will stop
While Joe will empty large bins
Up from the pizza shop

They Let Him Hold Me

These days I'm a loner
Make music no more
Think back when we started
In Kent Guitar Store

He came in for browsing
Young with attitude
Had gigged and got paid so
In purchasing mood

He played music with me
And he felt it too
You can't doubt that feeling
Just something we knew

Soon out on the road
Our crowds grew in size
Some wild, crazy parties
Some loves, some goodbyes

Some plane rides, some fighting
Some rock, and some blues
Some hotels, some mansions
Some headlining news

His fingers felt right on
My neck, never wrong
And fans loved us when we
Would play our best song

On that last day with him
The doctor agreed
We all knew the score and
They let him hold me

I like watching diners
Their burgers and fries
To some I'm expected
To some a surprise

There's some wouldn't know me
Their interest elsewhere
Some dragged by a partner
And just wouldn't care

I'm on Hard Rock's wall now
Guitar framed with pride
Some come just to see me
'Cause I never died

Working The Room

It's Sully here
Adept pub hound
Andy has beer
I'm looking round

I try to do
From near his stool
What they teach you
At puppy school

I catch their eye
And hang my head
I look like I
Am never fed

They stroke my ear
And take their seats
I saunter near
Yay! Got some treats!

Easter Parade

This bank hol sees varied people

Some are celebrating Easter

Some shop on their days off work

Then pester some poor barista

Some invite relations round

They're known as the family feaster

Me I'm best described as the

Hoping-for-five-eggs-at-leaster

Any Sutton

Tribute acts appear for
Artists you admire
So I'm "Any Sutton"
Poetry for hire

If you have a function
Budget is quite tight
I'll turn up and read as
Andy Sutton light

Doing things like myself
Might be hard to tell
Reading out my words but
Just not quite as well

Sounding quite authentic
Dressed just like real me
And all this for just a
Very modest fee

Talking To People I Don't Really Know

I'm talking to you at this open mic night
I might go down badly or might do alright
I've nothing to lose here so let's wait and see
'Cause I don't know you, and you don't know me

We're meeting at work because you are my boss
It's business as normal, no one gives a toss
My feelings, your feelings, we'll never agree
'Cause I don't know you, and you don't know me

I'm teaching you students I've plenty to say
As long as you're learning I'm doing okay
No need for connection or sharing a view
'Cause you don't know me, and I don't know you

Please help me doctor I'm not feeling well
Can I have some pills 'cause I'm ill you can tell
Just look at my notes is all you need to do
'Cause you don't know me, and I don't know you

Hello there my lover the rent's due today
Kids are at gran's where she's letting them play
I'm going out later, I've someone to see
'Cause I don't know you, and you don't know me

Pick A Number

Pick a number
Now add four
Subtract seven
Add three more
Workers suffer
Things get sore
Let a Tory
Through the door
Their solution
Change the law
Strikes get worse it
Feels like war
High inflation
Prices soar
Real wage tumbles
To the floor
Number, country
Tot the score
You're back where you
Were before

Blood Test Results

"Be Positive" said doctor

I dared not ask the rest

That answer made me anxious

Just after my blood test

"Should I now change my diet?

Switch to healthy soup?"

"Ha ha" said she "you've got me wrong!

"I told you your blood group!"

Colouring In

Here is seven year old Paul
He's not looking up at all
Colouring book on his knee
Showing things he'd like to be
Astronaut, farmer, teacher
Doctor, mechanic, preacher
Felt tip pens in plastic case
Concentration on his face
Pressing harder than he needs
Through the page the colour bleeds
Total focus in his mind
Tries to stay inside the lines
Colouring in

Thirty seven year old Paul
He's not looking up at all
Office rules for all to see
Dictate how it has to be
Tidy work without mistake
No fun, thinking, and no break
Eyes on that computer screen
Seeing what the numbers mean
Working harder than he needs
Brain feels sometimes like it bleeds
Total usage of his mind
Tries to stay inside the lines
Colouring in

A Disorderly Poem

*Inspired by the classic Two Ronnies sketch in which the answers
come before the questions*

Michael Flatley, Riverdancer

Question will come after answer

Which comes first the Q or A?

"D"'s the answer I will say

Name a thing we say is fourth

Anywhere that's facing north

What's good for shade loving plants?

Always wear clean underpants

What advice comes from your mum?

Whisky, vodka, brandy, rum

Name some booze you can drink neat

Name a man with rhythmic feet

My Dog Has No Nose

My dog's name was Rover
And he was very tame
And when I called him over
Rover always came
He liked to sniff the mower
The grass smelt good I s'pose
His head got ever lower
Then my dog had no nose
Then I called Rover over
He heeded to my call
Then someone shouts "How does he smell"
"Terrible" shouted one and all

We went to town one morning
And in the butcher's shop
He jumped up without warning
On to the counter top
The thing that tasted nicer
On which some meat was hung
Was the bacon slicer
Then my dog had no tongue
Then I called Rover over
He heeded to my call
Then someone shouts "How does he taste"
"Terrible" shouted one and all

Without his vital senses
The strain began to show
He used to jump on fences
And think he was a crow
He'd flap his legs and start to shake
If he saw bees or flies

Fell onto the garden rake
Then my dog had no eyes
Then I called Rover over
He heeded to my call
Then someone shouts "How does he look"
"Terrible" shouted one and all

The vet said little Rover's ills
And stings and aches would stay
Prescribed him rest and bright red pills
With food just once per day
They'd stop him feeling pains he'd got
Just what my dog deserves
He found and swallowed all the lot
Then my dog had no nerves
Then I called Rover over
He heeded to my call
Then someone shouts "How does he feel"
"Terrible" shouted one and all

Now Rover still could hear me
He'd prick his ears up high
He walked always quite near me
With our cat quite close by
The cat had just one minor vice
He'd eat just what appears
And dogs' ears look like little mice
Then my dog had no ears
Then I called Rover over
But he didn't come …

Head Held Still

Sam is hugged by a short

Slim white

Friday night

Knitted dress

From the bus stop to the Bull's Head

The pink ends of her blonde hair are

Untroubled by the breeze

While the band blasts

Sam blends

Until

She glides in front of the stage

Eyes closed

Trusting the dress

Her hands clasped above her head

Held still above her moving hips

Not dancing like nobody's watching

But dancing like everyone is

There's a band break

There's Steve

Who buys her a drink

Who moves on to a younger woman

Who leaves with the younger woman

Before the drum kit kicks off part two

Sam eyes an older man

But only his eyes

Are truly available

Back home

Sam slams shut the door

And drops her disappointed dress

Into the laundry

Children 1: Where We First Started

Sneaking early from your bed
Six years old fun in your head
Just for me on Fathers' Day
Spilled over a breakfast tray
Bowl of biscuits soaked in squash
I smile eating while you watch

On a train now me and you
Twelve years old with fun to do
Early morning London bound
Off-peak saver train seats found
You are listing where to shop
Picking out our lunchtime stop

Oxford Street is where we'll head
Endless clothes stores which I dread
Lots of browsing but few buys
Hide the glazed look from my eyes
Hiding but I think you see
Not the dad I'd like to be
One who'd like to shop with you
For your clothes and make up too
Hide from you that I look twice
At that crazy t-shirt price
You ask what might go with green
But you find my choice obscene
Your head gives a weary shake
Yet more shops no coffee break
Not sure I can stay good hearted
When we're back where we first started

Children 2: A Real Dad

Son I want to make amends
Since you're grown and we are friends
Sorry now that you are older
I pulled out of joint your shoulder
I'm a disappointing dad
You were just a normal lad
With consent I'll share some tales
Not all dads are alpha males

On Top Gear I never knew
Ford from BMW
You banned me from near your school
Skodas were just too uncool
Browsing then for my next car
You hoped for a Jaguar
Not your choice for motor heaven
Boring Peugeot two oh seven

Football talk I can't do much
All of sport I'm out of touch
So that time with some relations
When it was rugby Six Nations
You and cousin running round
In the living room you found
Me as you would rarely catch
Watching England's rugby match
Beer in hand and sporty chat
News to you I could do that
You said words you never had
"Wow you look like a real dad!"

Comparing Dogs With Children

Dogs are just nothing like children

Dogs spread out, filling your chairs

Dogs just go past and don't notice

Things that need taking upstairs

Dogs make you laugh when you're angry

Dogs do not put away toys

Dogs pester when you are sleepy

Dogs break the peace with their noise

Dogs bring in mud from the garden

Dogs do not put back on lids

Now having typed this I realise

Dogs are exactly like kids

Dragons' Den

On Dragons' Den that's on TV
Some business owners pitch
To get some funding to expand
In hopes of getting rich

I've got inventions in my head
That could just catch their eye
I'll sell my house and pawn my car
That's how hard I will try

Weary on your way to bed
Toothpaste flavour wanted most
Zingy, wake up, minty fresh?
No, sleepy Sunday roast

And sat nav voices of celebs
Are rather useless too
Mine will use the accent of
The place you're driving through

Coronation Suite

Written at the time of the coronation of King Charles

The Palace was keen to announce it

And some have been keen to denounce it

Pronouncement of king

Why's that a big thing?

It's really not hard to pronounce it

The crown that they put on his head

Is priceless and heavy as lead

He might think it's still a

Fun thing with Camilla

If one night he wears it in bed

The carriage watched by the armed forces

Has air con according to sources

He'll want some fresh air

We all would in there

For it's towed by eight gas-passing horses

Not Fitting In

Ten years since I

Came from outside

There's this pub

Where I reside

And in this place

Of local pride

It matters not

How much I've tried

I must have traits

They can't abide

I must have scars

I need to hide

Am I too tall?

Am I too wide?

It's clear that I

Won't fit inside

Dog Heirs

Dog heirs they get everywhere
On the window sill
In your cupboards, on the bed
In the bath, until
Finally when dad dog dies
They contest the will

Dog airs they get everywhere
I hear them all day
Rover plays the Irish flute
Like he's James Galway
Gentle ditties round the house
Folk is his forte

Dog hairs they get everywhere
Damn them! Such a curse!
On the carpets, on my clothes
Couldn't be much worse
So annoyed they've popped up now
Right here in this verse

Don't Put Anything In The Bin, I've Just Emptied It

Foretelling the future Mum knew all the lore
"What goes to the floor, well it comes to the door"
This was her wisdom should I drop a spoon
Cornflakes getting soggy I'd hope it came soon
Would it slink up the path, at the door ring the bell?
Quite how this would happen she never did tell

Another predictor was where we would itch
Her knowledge of body parts endlessly rich
Palms would mean money she had us believe
If left you were giving but right to receive
My favourite itch less specific than some
Was "Itchy bum? Surprise to come."

While watching Olympians going for gold
A gymnast scored "perfect" while not very old
To help Olga answer that medal hope call
I guess that her parents had given their all
Surveying the front room in which us kids sat
Mum said "Why can't you lot be clever like that?"

And now as a dad I just cannot compete
I don't know the meaning of their itchy feet
But one thing survived that I found myself saying
When my two had rubbish from eating or playing
As well brought up kids they are trained they should bin it
"I just emptied that don't put anything in it"

But First I Need To …

I'd better just clean out the fish tank

The dog needs to have a long walk

That cupboard is overdue sorting

I should phone my sister in York

Look at that dust on the hi-fi

My kitchen floor can't stay like that

The bookshelf needs putting in order

My bike tyres both look a bit flat

I'm really not procrastinating

It's not that I'm trying to shirk

It's just that these things must be dealt with

And then I can get on with work

May Day

I may paint my bedroom
Pick a shade of grey
I may fit those curtains
Yes perhaps I may

I may write a new scene
Finish off that play
I may get it published
Yes this time I may

I may start a hobby
Learn to work with clay
I may go to classes
Yes I think I may

I may just be lazy
Back to bed and stay
Lots of things to do but
Maybe not today

Belong

I wish I was not allowed to

 Stream that old jazz song

I wish I was mad a spoon was

 Where the forks belong

I wish that there wasn't room to

 Stretch out in my bed

I wish that there wasn't time to

 Get my emails read

I wish I'd get up and freeze to

 Make your cup of tea

What I'd give to be annoyed that

 You were here with me

Returning The Carriage

If I put carriage returns
Randomly
Into a
Sentence
Is it
Then
A poem?
Can I
Do it mid wo
Rd?
Will a
Glittering
Adjective save the day?
Is my poem always prized so
Long as I
Write about my
Personal
Feelings
My emotional vulnerability
With no
New insights
And no word craft
Except the
Bloody
Carriage returns

Reasons To Be Cheerful, Part Me

Weekend breaks
Eating cakes
Well picked words
Grammar nerds
Counting Crows
Days it snows
Bakewell tart
Dali's art
Holding hands
Local bands
Local pubs
Shoulder rubs
Maths and stats
(weird one that)
Stressing less
Songs by Yes
Pink Floyd prog
Sully Dog
Grass cut smells
Plus ... Tubular Bells

Sunny days
Clever plays
Funny vids
My two kids
Merlot sips
Caustic quips
Daytime naps
O.S. maps
Wine cork pops
Chocolate drops
Bumper crops
Brewing hops
Gadget shops
Lucky Chops
Coffee stops
Sofa flops
and
Spending time
Writing rhyme

Honesty

The number of calls we are currently dealing with is completely normal, but we don't have enough staff or resources to help you without a long wait. It's never any quicker than this, and we are not going to pretend that this is an unusually high volume of calls right now.

You can achieve anything if you believe. Unless there are:
-Limitations in your skills and abilities
-Structural inequalities in your society
-Time constraints
-Competing demands in your life
-Aggressive and competitive people who get in your way
-Random events that get in your way
-People who try harder than you
-Insufficient resources
-Needier people who you decide to help instead of chasing your own goals
-Unrealistic aspects of your ambitions

Our store loyalty card is not intended to reward you for your loyalty in shopping with us, which we could do just by reducing prices at the till. It is designed to track you and your shopping habits so that we know how to tempt you into spending more.

I will not fill in my dating site profile later.

Although you can download our software for free, or create an account for free, here is the price we'll charge you if you want to use it.

Your parcel was not 'handed to resident', it was dropped somewhere near your doorstep after a short knock on your door immediately before the driver walked away.

We have no plans to raise taxes. We also have no plans to go to bed tonight, but both things are likely to happen.

I have not read or understood any of the terms and conditions before continuing.

The concept of trickledown economics was invented as a joke, but we found some people sort of believed it, so we're just going to see how long we can get away with it.

A Family Of Limericks

There once was a Limerick dad
His wife, and three verse kids they had
To try to make money
They had to be funny
Though deep down inside they were sad

For instance a hard thing for mum
Undignified rhyme was to come
These two lines were chiefly
To put it off briefly
But then it all ended with "bum"

The angst ridden teen bore a curse
And thought that life couldn't be worse
Not knowing what "nice" is
Existential crisis
No hope of life outside this verse

The next child's distress was deflected
Not quite as upset as expected
As child in between
And not yet a teen
Unfunny rhyme went undetected

The youngest child while still quite small
Had started before they could scrawl
In quite a short time
They figured out rhyme
But hadn't got the hang of scansion or meter at all

Low Tech

At the cop shop still they lurk

Monitors that people gave her

Doesn't matter if they work

She's a keen PC screen saver

On the bus Tim never rests

New job on a double decker

Giving out the Covid tests

Latest mobile virus checker

Sorry if they tend to fatten

Broth or pastries served today

Laid out in a special pattern

The in-formation soup or pie way

Shopping In York

I went into York centre
For jeans, of which I'm fond
I came back with a postcard and
A Harry Potter wand

Next day I wanted brackets
A shelf had fallen down
I bought a bar walls pencil and
A Harry Potter gown

I sought a larger dog bed
My hound is getting bigger
I bought a new fridge magnet and
A Harry Potter figure

I looked for some emulsion
To decorate the flat
I got a Betty's cream cake and
A Harry Potter hat

Some glue was on my list next
My shoe heel split in half
Got pork pies from The Shambles and
A Harry Potter scarf

I needed some new curtains
The ones I had were fowl
Purchased a model Minster and
A Harry Potter owl

Urgently seeking lotion
Been bitten by a bug
Got plastic Viking helmets and
A Harry Potter mug

New boots because it's winter
I'm looking for size ten
Got soft vanilla fudge and
A Harry Potter pen

My son's eleventh birthday
A book would do no doubt
Something by JK Rowling but
The shops had all sold out

Never

Never send your child to school if you know they have
   lice

Never save your takeaway and then reheat the rice

Never lift a weight up and forget to bend your legs

Never count your chickens up when they are merely eggs

Never interrupt your foe who's making a mistake

Never eat then try to swim without a decent break

Never drive while drunk and also never jump red lights

Never cross a picket line or question workers' rights

Never shoot the messenger for news they have to break

Never chill red wine and never overcook the steak

Never run with scissors that you're holding in your hand

Never start your sentences with "but", "because", or
   "and"

Never shop while hungry if you'll be at the food store

Never eat the yellow snow where dogs have been before

Never with a crocodile should you attempt a smile

Never double denim if you care about your style

Never eat the last Rolo when out with chocoholics

Never Gonna Give You Up, and Never Mind The
  Bollocks

Never talk when dining if in your mouth food still lingers

Never step on pavement cracks unless you cross your
  fingers

Never drop an "h" though it's OK while saying "honour"

Never talk to strangers or you might end up a goner

Never judge a book by simply looking at its cover

Never spend the night before a match bedding your lover

Never drink so much that you lose track of where the
  floor is

Never, never, never, no don't ever trust the Tories

Artificial Intelligence

I asked the A.I. to write me some lines

Cod was the topic selected to air

Half of these creatures were just philistines

No sense of style and so unaware

That half of the shoal wore ill-fitting clothes

Saying so little of relevance

Half of them though they were stylish – it shows

Arty fish'll hint elegance

Just Chicken

Stopped to buy some lunch today
A meal deal works for me
A drink, a snack, and sandwich
Which filling will it be?

Cheese and pickle, ham, or egg
And then there's B.L.T.
Pulled pork, salad, prawn mayo
"Just Chicken", yes, maybe

After all I would not like
A bird that was unfair
With no sense of right and wrong
When in a judges chair

Or do they mean something else?
Is testing now a must
Checking hen identity
It passed but only just

Diabolical Struggles

Satan popped in recently
I guess just on his rounds
Wondered if I'd sell my soul
For seven hundred pounds

"Seven million!" I replied
He said "Meet in the middle
That's my offer nowadays
Unless you play the fiddle?"

"Not that tempting" countered I
"Can't you be more realistic?
Give me something highly prized
Or magical and mystic?"

Blaming brimstone going up
While sulphur costs are rising
Fire insurance rates so steep
And pricey advertising

He said that if things don't change
He'll have to change profession
Maybe even switching sides
Recruiting souls for heaven

Fatherly Dilemma

My eldest shared a video

Wine bottle in his hands

He necks the whole lot down in one

And afterwards still stands

Should I now disapprove by text

Signed "very worried dad"

Or hold his hand aloft and cry

"Well done now, that's my lad!"?

Life Cycle

Work started at age twenty two
Helping when life had gone wrong
The mother with rent overdue
The man who'd been homeless too long

Samantha would make it OK
Days away walking on sand
She sang as they drank chardonnay
She had eyes that said "I understand"

Tim's days they were getting more tough
Needing Sam's hugs, just to mend
Helping those still sleeping rough
His work made him nobody's friend

There were signs he denied
He was dad she was mother
Though they really had tried
Sam had turned to another

His work became too much to do
Sam's gone and sings a new song
Tim struggles with rent overdue
And homelessness won't be too long

End Of My Book

So here you are at the end of my book

I am so thankful that you've had a look

Did you just jump here to see how it ends?

Like a whodunnit with murderous trends?

Or did you get here but missed one or two?

Or did you skip over more than a few?

Maybe you started then read every page?

Would you like others at some future stage?

If you enjoyed it please leave a review

If not I'm sorry I distracted you

Please get in touch if you've something to say

I will reply in a most grateful way

Andy

Printed in Great Britain
by Amazon

23126275R00050